FEB 2 1 2006

W9-AVO-176

WITHDRAWN

PROPERTY OF
Kankakee Public Library

WITHDRAWN

THE LIBRARY OF
EMERGENCY PREPAREDNESS™

TERRORIST ATTACKS

A PRACTICAL SURVIVAL GUIDE

Kerry Hinton

rosen
central™

The Rosen Publishing Group, Inc., New York

Published in 2006 by The Rosen Publishing Group, Inc.
29 East 21st Street, New York, NY 10010

Copyright © 2006 by The Rosen Publishing Group, Inc.

First Edition

All rights reserved. No part of this book may be reproduced in any form
without permission in writing from the publisher, except by a reviewer.

Library of Congress Cataloging-in-Publication Data

Hinton, Kerry.
Terrorist attacks: a practical survival guide / by Kerry Hinton.—1st ed.
    p. cm.—(The library of emergency preparedness)
Includes bibliographical references and index.
ISBN 1-4042-0529-2 (lib. bdg.)
1. Terrorism. 2. Emergency management—United States.
I. Title. II. Series.
HV6431.H543 2006
363.35—dc22

                                                      2005013893

Manufactured in Malaysia.

On the cover: People run for their lives as the south tower of the World
Trade Center in New York City comes crashing down after the deadly terrorist attacks of September 11, 2001.

3 1558 00222 3626

CONTENTS

Introduction

The events of September 11, 2001, made every United States citizen aware of the danger posed by terrorist attacks. The governments of the United States and many countries around the world acknowledged the emergence of a new and dangerous threat: global terrorism.

Unfortunately, the possibility of terrorists and terrorist groups hurting people and spreading fear is not at all new. For centuries, groups with extreme political beliefs have made use of terrorist tactics to threaten governments or achieve other goals. Terrorists believe in their cause so strongly that they are willing to not only harm others, but sacrifice their own lives as well.

Terrorism was common in the United States from the latter half of the nineteenth century to the beginning of the twentieth century. Terrorists detonated bombs at the financial center of New York City in 1920, attempting to disrupt the nation's economy. A group known as the Ku Klux Klan used violence and fear to further its goal of white supremacy.

Unfortunately, goals and methods of terrorists are not easy to explain. Terrorism is a broad and complex idea that is not limited to any single country, culture, race, religion, or individual.

This photograph was taken only seconds after United Airlines Flight 175 struck the south tower of the World Trade Center at approximately 9:00 AM on September 11, 2001. Debris from the skyscraper can be seen falling to the street below.

This book will tell you what you can do to prepare for a terrorist attack, and what you need to do if one occurs. We'll look at some helpful information on how to prepare mentally and physically for such attacks, as well as how to deal with their aftereffects.

The United States Federal Code of Regulations classifies terrorism as "The unlawful use of force and violence against persons or property to intimidate a government, the civilian population, or any segment thereof, in furtherance of political or social objectives." In short, terrorist acts are motivated in the hope of causing some sort of change in leadership, laws, or policies.

Types of Terrorism

Domestic terrorism occurs when people from a nation or state commit terrorist acts against their fellow citizens. Planning, funding, manpower, and the implementation of a domestic terrorist attack all take place in the country that is being targeted. Examples of this would be the Oklahoma City, Oklahoma bombing of 1995 and the Tokyo, Japan, subway gas attack of 1995. Both attacks were carried out by citizens of their respective countries.

International terrorism is not limited to the boundaries of a particular nation. It involves individuals or groups from one or multiple nations who decide to take action against another country. The attacks on the World Trade Center in 1993 and 2001 are well-known examples of international terrorism. Despite the fact that much of the planning and training for both attacks occurred in the United States, the direction and motivation for the crimes originated out-side of the United States.

State-sponsored terrorism occurs in two ways. The first may be the most disturbing type of terrorism because it involves a government using terrorist tactics against its own people. For example, if a government wishes to stop a potential rebellion or to maintain order, it may resort to harming its citizens in order to achieve this goal. Another aspect of state-sponsored terrorism occurs when a government offers protection from prosecu-tion to known terrorists or assists in the training, operations, or funding of terrorist groups.

The most crucial point to remember is that terrorism does not occur randomly. No matter what the act may be, planning is completely necessary to terrorist activities. Hence, a violent crime committed spontaneously cannot be considered to be a terrorist act.

Does Terrorism Work?

Sadly, in many cases, the answer is yes. Even if the original goal of a terrorist or terrorist group is not fully reached, these attacks often have disastrous consequences. The 2001 attacks on the World Trade Center and Pentagon demon-strate this. In addition to causing nearly 3,000 deaths, the attacks of September 11 created severe economic problems for the United States. The New York Stock Exchange closed for the first time since the Great Depression of 1933, and when it reopened six days later, the Dow Jones stock index fell almost 700 points—its largest drop ever. In total, stocks in the United States lost more than $1 trillion in value over the

Emergency workers survey the terrible destruction caused by the bombing of the Alfred P. Murrah Federal Building in Oklahoma City, Oklahoma, on April 19, 1995. One hundred and sixty-eight people lost their lives when American-born terrorist Timothy McVeigh detonated a truck full of explosives outside the building. McVeigh was eventually convicted for his crimes and received the death penalty.

next week. In addition, the airline industry experienced a large decrease in ticket sales due to fears of terrorism.

On an individual level, the families of the business-people, firefighters, and police officers killed that day were thrown into complete chaos. Many New Yorkers and visitors to the city who witnessed the attacks began to suffer from a condition known as post-traumatic stress disorder (PTSD). This disorder, which is the result of undergoing severe trauma, is usually experienced by soldiers who have been in battle. The symptoms of PTSD include anxiety, fear, a loss of emotional sensitivity, and vivid nightmares. PTSD can also be responsible for many other debilitating physical and psychological side effects.

The plans of many potential terrorists are foiled by the United States and other governments around the world. However, to be safe, especially since we know the damage even one successful attempt can accomplish, we need to be aware of the danger of terrorist attacks and prepare ourselves accordingly.

2 --- General Emergency Preparations

"Let our advance worrying become advance thinking and planning."

—Winston Churchill

Worrying about terrorist attacks is not very practical. Being prepared by planning for an attack is much more useful. While the men and women who work for government offices such as the Federal Bureau of Investigation (FBI) and the Department of Homeland Security are working hard to keep the United States safe, the average person can do his or her part by making some basic preparations and knowing what do before, during, and after an attack.

The Department of Homeland Security was created in 2002 to coordinate many of the organizations that aid in the fight against domestic terror. This government agency also helps educate the public on emergency preparedness and emergency action. Combining the skills and advice of these different groups resulted in the National Response Plan. The plan contains an "all-hazards approach," incorporating the best advice and procedures from the fields of law enforcement, fire fighting, and other areas that may be needed in case of a catastrophe.

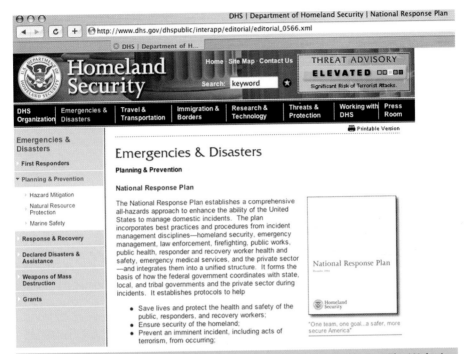

This is a page from the Department of Homeland Security's Web site. The Web site contains news, facts, and tips on how to prepare for a potential terrorist attack. There is also important information regarding travel, transportation, immigration, borders, and threats to the American public. Contact information is made available for citizens with questions or concerns regarding their safety.

One of the most important innovations of the Department of Homeland Security is the Homeland Security Advisory System, which issues the Threat Advisory Level. This five-color system is usually updated daily. It estimates the risk of a terror attack, ranging from "low" to "severe." Each risk level has a corresponding recommendation for individual and family planning. Checking the daily threat level may be a good first step for your personal emergency plan. Many news channels announce it daily, and it can always

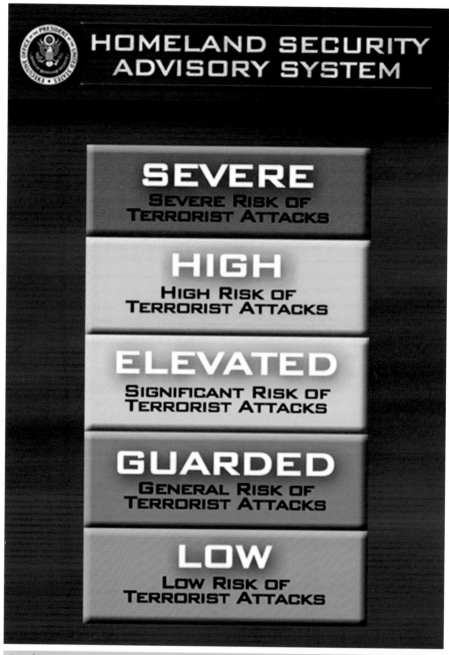

HOMELAND SECURITY
ADVISORY SYSTEM

SEVERE
SEVERE RISK OF
TERRORIST ATTACKS

HIGH
HIGH RISK OF
TERRORIST ATTACKS

ELEVATED
SIGNIFICANT RISK OF
TERRORIST ATTACKS

GUARDED
GENERAL RISK OF
TERRORIST ATTACKS

LOW
LOW RISK OF
TERRORIST ATTACKS

As of 2005, the Threat Advisory Level has never been elevated to red. It has also not been reduced to blue or green since its inception in 2002. The decision to raise or lower the Threat Advisory Level is made on a case-by-case basis.

be found on the Department of Homeland Security Web site at http://www.dhs.gov.

Your Emergency Plan

The Federal Emergency Management Association (FEMA) is the arm of the Department of Homeland Security that is specifically concerned with emergency planning and preparedness. FEMA publishes a helpful (and free) manual entitled "Are You Ready? An In-Depth Guide to Citizen Preparedness," which takes readers through a variety of emergency situations and offers common-sense advice on preparing for a disaster.

There is no definitive format for an emergency plan, and each person's plan will vary. The only requirement is that the plan cover some basic actions that should be taken well in advance of an attack to ensure preparedness. Since one doesn't necessarily know when an attack will occur, you should develop an emergency plan sooner rather than later. Being informed is one of the most important aspects of an emergency plan. Having all the answers is not necessary, but knowing where to get them may be. Some things you should consider when developing your basic emergency plan are:

1. Know which radio and television stations in your area are a part of the Emergency Broadcast System. In the event of a disaster, this network of stations will give regional or nationwide information, including safe areas, evacuation routes, and general information the state or federal government may need to communicate

to citizens. In certain cases, many travel routes may be blocked off for security or safety. Always follow the directions local and national authorities give following a terrorist attack.

2. Have a communications plan. A cell phone is a great way to communicate with friends and family members if service hasn't been affected by an attack. This plan includes knowing the phone numbers of friends, family members, and medical personnel. Nonetheless, even with a cell phone, one must consider alternative means of communications. For example, the attacks of September 11 disrupted cell phone service for a large number of people in New York City, leaving many people to rely on local phone service.

3. An escape route is also an important aspect of an emergency plan. Planning multiple routes is very helpful. Know all of the ways to get in and out of your home, since some exits may be blocked. If it is not safe to enter your home, you and your family should have one or two alternate meeting places.

4. Have some emergency funds at your disposal. If power has been disrupted, some automated teller machines (ATMs) may not work. You should always have some cash on hand, in case you need to purchase food or other supplies.

5. Take a first-aid or CPR (cardiopulmonary resuscitation) course. You may want to find out where the local American Red Cross holds courses. The ability

These two Chicago-area high school students are being instructed on how to use a defibrillator as part of a CPR-training session. A defibrillator is a medical device used to get a person's heart beating after a cardiac arrest. It does this by giving the heart an electric shock. It has been responsible for saving many lives.

to save or prolong a life after a tragedy is an invaluable skill.

As you may not be at home during a terrorist attack, you should ask about the emergency plans at your school or workplace. Your school's plan should cover evacuation, emergency food and water, and shelter. One final note: instead of putting your emergency plan in a drawer and forgetting it, pull it out occasionally and review it. Make sure you're familiar with your meeting places and evacuation plans. Should an emergency arise, advance preparation could save your life.

YOUR EMERGENCY KIT

The Red Cross recommends that the basic emergency kit contain at least the following items:

✓ **Flashlight** For situations when the power is out. Make sure you have batteries, and DO NOT substitute candles in the event that there may be explosive gases in the air. Be sure to check the batteries to make sure they are charged.

✓ **Battery-powered radio** For any emergency broadcasts. There are also some wind-up radios on the market that do not require batteries or electrical power.

✓ **Plastic sheeting and duct tape** In certain chemical, biological, and radiation attacks, evacuation may not be advised. These two items are to be used to cover windows and doors securely to prevent dangerous toxins from entering a space if you are unable to leave.

✓ **Food** Store food at school or a workplace. One day of food is recommended. The Red Cross defines a one-day food supply as three meals. At home, three days' worth of food is suggested. Avoid salty foods that may make you thirsty or food that may spoil quickly (fresh fruit, raw meat). Suitable items include canned fruits, meats, and juices, as well as energy bars or other nonperishable foods.

✓ **Water** It is crucial to have water in an emergency kit. One gallon (3.8 liters) of water (kept in plastic and not glass or cardboard) should be the minimum amount on hand.

✓ **Medication** Keep at least three days' worth of prescription medicine in any type of emergency kit. Also keep nonprescription medicine, such as aspirin or other pain relievers.

✓ **First-aid supplies** The Red Cross Web site (http://www.redcross.org) has a full list of first-aid equipment that you should include in your emergency kit.

Your Emergency Kit

In the event of an attack, you may not be able to return home immediately. Depending on the type and severity of the attack, you may have to survive on your own or with a few people in a space where basic essentials such as food, water, and fresh air may not be readily available. Having a portable emergency kit can be extremely helpful and potentially life-saving in these situations. "Portable" is the key word here—if a disaster strikes, being able to move quickly is very important.

The American Red Cross provides invaluable advice that will help you build your emergency kit. Additionally, it is a good idea to have more than one kit for various locations where you may find yourself, such as home, school, and work. Emergency kits in various sizes are available for purchase from the American Red Cross, but you can obtain all of the items in the Red Cross kit on your own.

Think about personalizing your emergency preparedness kit. If you wear glasses or contact lenses, you may want to have one or more extra pairs in workplace or school kits and at home. You may also want to include a change of clothes (account for warm and cold weather) or an extra pair of shoes, for instance.

FEMA and the Red Cross offer information on emergency planning and emergency kits on their respective Web sites, which are noted at the end of this book.

Knowing how to prepare for a general emergency is important, but there are still many things you should know that are specific to terrorist attacks. We will examine the ways in which terrorists and terror groups carry out their attacks, the methods they prefer, and what to do after an attack. Every threat is different and may require some unique action.

3 --- Explosives

At present, explosives are the most frequent means of attack used by terrorists. This is in part because they are relatively inexpensive when compared to chemical, biological, and nuclear weapons. Not only do they cause death and destruction quickly, but the loud and chaotic nature of explosive devices can effectively cause a large degree of fear and psychological damage far away from the actual blast. Bombs have been used on churches, important monuments, public buildings, and financial institutions. Regardless of property damage, it's important to know that the majority of terrorists use them for one purpose: to injure or kill people.

Types of Explosive Devices

There are many different types of explosive devices. They can be as small as a grenade or large enough to fill the back of a moving van. Most explosives can be divided into the following groups.

- **Pipe bombs** As the name suggests, these devices consist of explosive material stuffed into a pipe of metal or plastic. Pipe bombs can be set off via remote control or with a timer. They are very easy to manufacture.

A police officer in Belfast, Northern Ireland, shows a bag full of pipe bombs. Terrorism in Northern Ireland has been a big problem since the late 1960s. The tension between the country's Protestant and Catholic populations has led to many acts of violence.

- **Vehicle bombs** A large version of the pipe bomb. A car or truck is packed with explosives and detonated. Vehicle bombs are intended to cause as much destruction as possible.

- **Letter and package bombs** These are bombs concealed in letters or parcels that often explode when opened. The most notorious instance of letter bombing in the United States was undertaken by Ted Kaczynski (known as the Unabomber). His efforts killed three people and injured twenty-nine, over a seventeen-year period.

- **Unconventional bombs** These devices can take many forms, from a bomb detonated by a suicide bomber, to the attacks of September 11, 2001, in which aircrafts were hijacked and used as bombs themselves. Dirty bombs also fall into this category.

Is an Explosive Attack Likely?

The attacks of September 11 and Oklahoma City demonstrate that an explosive attack is the most likely form of terrorism to be expected. Explosives remain an attractive option to people who wish to inflict harm on a group of people.

The materials for making bombs are quite easy to obtain. The bomb that rocked the Alfred P. Murrah Federal Building in Oklahoma City was made using almost 5,000 pounds (2,268 kilograms) of fertilizer and diesel fuel oil. Most hardware stores sell items that can be fashioned into explosive devices. It is very easy for a potential terrorist to acquire bomb-making materials. Since we know that the possibility of explosive attacks are a reality, we should discuss what actions to take when they occur.

How to Handle an Explosive Attack

It is important to always be aware of your environment. Be familiar with the escape routes outlined in your family or personal emergency plan. When you enter a building, check for emergency exits and staircases. If you are in a building that is attacked, you'll need to know where these exits are. As with all attacks, the first step is to get away from the site of the incident as soon as you can.

If you are outside and an explosion occurs, you will need to evacuate the area for your own safety and to allow rescue crews to do their jobs. Additionally, some

EXPLOSIONS If there is an explosion...

Take shelter under your desk or a sturdy table.

Exit the building as quickly as possible.

Do not use elevators.

Check for fire and other hazards.

Take your emergency kit if time allows.

attacks may involve more than one explosion—be sure to avoid buildings that have a large number of glass windows and doors.

If you are inside and close to the explosion, you may need to find temporary shelter until it is safe to leave. Remember to try to stay calm and be on the lookout for damage on your exit route. If there is a fire, try to keep as low to the ground as you can to avoid inhaling smoke. In some cases, you may not be able to leave a building. If you cannot escape from where you are, do your best to protect your lungs by covering your nose and mouth until help arrives. Try not to yell for help. Many building materials can become toxic after an explosion, and you may inhale some of these vapors or particles. Look for items you can use to alert people to your whereabouts. If you have a cellular

EXPLOSIONS If there is fire...

Exit the building as quickly as possible.

Crawl low in smoke.

Use a wet cloth to cover your nose and mouth.

phone, try to make a phone call. Be calm and give rescue personnel an accurate and detailed description of your location. Tapping on walls or piping can also be a good method of alerting rescue crews to where you are.

EXPLOSIONS If you are trapped in debris...

If possible, use a flashlight to signal your location.

Avoid unnecessary movement so that you don't kick up dust.

Cover your mouth and nose with anything you have on hand. Dense weave cotton material can create a good filter. Try to breathe through the material.

Tap on a pipe or wall so that rescuers can hear where you are.

Use a whistle if one is available. Shout only as a last resort - shouting can cause a person to inhale dangerous amounts of dust.

In many cases, the potential of terrorist attacks can be used to disturb the mental state and day-to-day lives of citizens and the government. If you happen to be notified of a bomb threat, always take it seriously. Tell someone in a position of authority and evacuate the suspect area as quickly as you can. Even if it turns out to be a false alarm or a prank, it's better to be safe than sorry.

4 --- Chemical Attacks

As with all types of terrorism, using chemicals to inflict damage on a civilian population or armed force is not a new idea. Chemical warfare first came to real prominence during World War I (1914–1918), when the French and British forces used tear gas on the German army. Other chemical weapons used during World War I, such as mustard gas, were extremely deadly. The use of chemical weapons has since been declared unlawful by the 1925 Geneva Protocal and the 1997 Chemical Weapons Convention.

Types of Chemical Agents

The correct term for chemicals used in warfare is "chemical agents." An agent is what a chemical weapon (a missile or rocket) carries or delivers. The agent is what does the intended damage. As with the varying types of terrorism, there are different classifications given to chemical agents. For our purposes, we can look at two major categories of chemical agents: nonlethal and lethal.

Nonlethal chemical agents are designed to temporarily incapacitate individuals, as opposed to killing them. An example of a nonlethal chemical agent is tear gas, which has been used in wartime and also in situations where riot control is required. Though tear gas can be lethal if too much is used in too small a space, it is still considered nonlethal because of its designated purpose. Other chemical agents that were not designed to kill have been used to destroy enemy crops (herbicides).

All chemical agents require a minimum concentration to be effective. If that concentration is not reached, the agent will not be as useful. The four major types of lethal chemical agents are:

- **Choking agents** These are also called asphyxiants or respiratory agents, since they negatively impact a person's ability to breathe. The most common examples

Members of the Holloman Air Force Base Hazardous Materials Response Unit 1 spray down a fellow airman. People in this line of work must wear special protective suits that cover their entire bodies. Exposure to certain chemical agents may cause sickness or death.

of this are chlorine gas and phosgene. Choking agents burn tissue in the lungs and cause a condition known as "dry land drowning."

- **Blister agents** This is the family in which mustard gas belongs. As the name suggests, blister agents cause painful burns and large blisters on the skin and eyes. Inhaling a blister agent can be fatal, burning the lungs and throat of the victim.

- **Blood agents** Blood agents perform the same task as choking agents, but at a much deeper level. A blood agent attacks human cells, rather than the lungs, and prevents respiration on a cellular level. Without the oxygen generated by this respiration, a person who breathes in a blood agent will suffocate.

This Iraqi mortar shell recovered by the Danish army in January 2004 was thought to contain a blister agent. However, tests later showed it did not. Iraq used chemical weapons in its war with Iran in the 1980s.

The most famous use of blood agents was in the Nazi concentration camps of World War II, where a type of gas called Zyklon B (whose active ingredient is hydrogen cyanide) was used. This could kill people in a small space within fifteen minutes. Americans who receive the death penalty and choose the gas chamber are put to death by means of cyanide, which is also a blood agent.

- **Nerve agents** Nerve agents are the most deadly type of chemical agents that exist. They require the small-est dosage to do the most damage and act much more quickly than any of the other three types. Nerve agents are colorless and usually odorless. Inhaling a nerve agent can cause death within fifteen minutes.

Japanese soldiers are seen here cleaning a Tokyo subway car after a fatal gas attack in 1995. Members of a Japanese cult called Aum Shinrikyo released sarin gas in the Tokyo subway system. Thousands of early morning commuters were seriously injured and twelve died after being exposed to the lethal nerve agent.

As a result of contact with skin, a nerve agent can kill a person in less than two minutes.

The nerve agent sarin is 500 times as powerful as cyanide. As with blood agents and choking agents, sarin causes suffocation. However, sarin does so by paralyzing the muscles in and around the lungs. Sarin was used in the Tokyo subway attacks of 1995, when members of the Aum Shinrikyo doomsday cult exposed thousands of commuters to the deadly substance. Sarin was also used by Iraqi dictator Saddam Hussein against Iraq's Kurdish population in 1987 to 1988.

VX may have the shortest name of any chemical agent, but it is the deadliest human-made chemical substance ever to be created. It exists as an oily liquid, and only a fraction of the lethal amount of sarin needed to kill is necessary. Additionally, VX is persistent, meaning that once it is used, it can contaminate an area for quite some time.

How Chemical Agents Are Used

"Delivery" is the term used for getting a chemical agent to its destination. Even though blood, blister, and choking agents are not very difficult to fabricate, delivering them usually poses a problem. Since chemical weapons had most commonly been used on the battlefield, a more widespread method of delivery was through explosives including bombs, mines, and grenades.

There are many alternative means of dispersing agents. Some are more effective and can reach a greater area when pressurized and released via aerosol (the same way hair spray is released) or through a large sprayer based on the ground or attached to an aircraft (similar to a crop duster). Chemical agents could also be used to contaminate a region's food or water supplies. Even if no one were injured, this would be a huge disruption in the lives of a great number of people.

Is a Chemical Attack Likely?

The difficulty of harming or killing a great number of people through a chemical attack may not make such an incident an ideal option for terrorists. However, that doesn't mean chemical attacks are unlikely to happen.

The most direct means of attack may do the most damage when chemical weapons are concerned. Consider the first chemical attack during World War I. The German army simply opened the valves on canisters of chlorine gas and managed to do a significant amount of damage in a relatively small area. In short, if a chemical attack takes place and you are not in the immediate area that has been affected, your chances for survival are relatively good.

How to Handle a Chemical Attack

It is not always evident when a chemical attack has taken place. Many chemical agents likely to be used in an attack are colorless and nearly odorless. The agents that do have odors (for example, hydrogen cyanide smells like bitter almonds and sarin has a faint fruity odor) are not as likely to be used if an organization wishes to create mass casualties. With some agents, it may take as long as forty-eight hours for symptoms to occur after exposure. If a bomb or explosive has not detonated, the first indication may be the symptoms associated with a particular chemical. Since most lethal chemicals

CHEMICAL THREAT

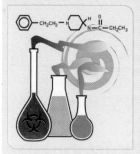

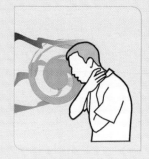

A chemical attack is the deliberate release of a toxic gas, liquid or solid that can poison people and the environment.

Watch for signs such as many people suffering from watery eyes, twitching, choking, having trouble breathing or losing coordination.

Many sick or dead birds, fish or small animals are also cause for suspicion.

If you see signs of a chemical attack, quickly try to define the impacted area or where the chemical is coming from, if possible.

Take immediate action to get away from any sign of a chemical attack.

If the chemical is inside a building where you are, try to get out of the building without passing through the contaminated area, if possible.

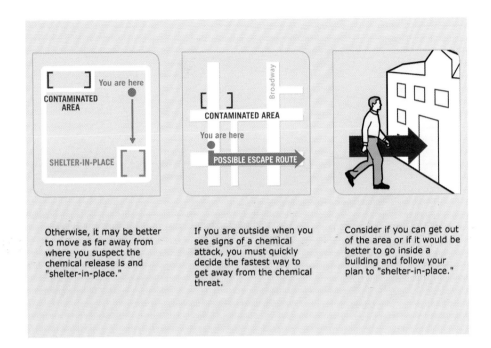

Otherwise, it may be better to move as far away from where you suspect the chemical release is and "shelter-in-place."

If you are outside when you see signs of a chemical attack, you must quickly decide the fastest way to get away from the chemical threat.

Consider if you can get out of the area or if it would be better to go inside a building and follow your plan to "shelter-in-place."

ultimately affect the lungs and respiration, breathing difficulties would be common. Other symptoms can range from a runny nose and red eyes to wheezing and giddiness, nausea, vomiting, and collapse. If you are outdoors, see how birds or other animals react, since chemical agents will also affect them. If you see an unusual cloud of smoke, fog, or sprays of vapor, leaving the area would be strongly advised. Also be aware of people wearing unusual clothing, including gas masks or other breathing aids.

Is it necessary to own a gas mask? Gas masks are incredibly helpful, but for one to be completely effective, you would have to be wearing it before an attack took place. Since we know the "invisible" nature of chemical warfare, this is very challenging. In addition, the mask should ideally be fitted to a person's face, and very few people can

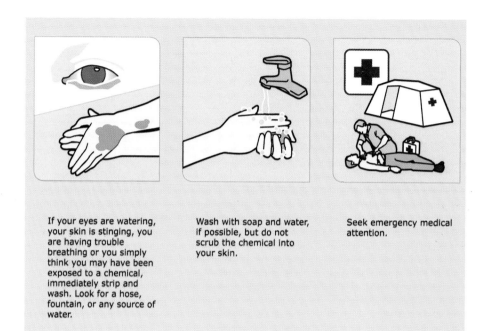

If your eyes are watering, your skin is stinging, you are having trouble breathing or you simply think you may have been exposed to a chemical, immediately strip and wash. Look for a hose, fountain, or any source of water.

Wash with soap and water, if possible, but do not scrub the chemical into your skin.

Seek emergency medical attention.

obtain custom-fit gas masks. The Red Cross does not recommend their use for the general public, most notably because people who own gas masks can acquire a false sense of security.

As in any disaster, the first thing to do if a chemical agent is released in your area is to remain calm. Panic will only decrease your chances of surviving the event. The next and most important step is to leave the area. Think about your emergency plan. You may have to figure out an escape route to get to fresh air. Your location will determine what to do next.

When you are inside, leaving shelter may not be a wise idea. Close all windows and doors. Shut off all air-conditioning or heating units so outside air cannot enter. Listen to the radio or watch television to find out the full scope of the attack. If authorities are giving instructions, be sure to follow them. People in high-rises or taller buildings should head for the highest ground possible; since chemical agents are heavier than air, higher altitudes will provide more safety. If you are in a car, stay inside. Shut all vents and windows and listen to the radio for further instructions. If you are at home and there has been a large-scale attack, use the plastic sheeting and duct tape in your emergency kit to seal off part of your home and create a safe space. Your space should have as few windows as possible, a telephone, and a bathroom. Be prepared for the possibility of staying there for a few days or more.

When you are outside, try to figure out from where the agent was released. If you can see anything (a cloud of smoke or gas), head upwind from that area. Remember, all lethal chemical agents damage airways, so keep your mouth and nose covered with a handkerchief or surgical mask as you leave the scene. Try not to use outer clothing (such as coats) since it may have traces of the agent. If you feel fine but think you may have been exposed, immediately remove all of your clothing, wash your hair and body with soap and water, flush your eyes if necessary, and seek medical attention.

5 --- Biological Attacks

Biological warfare is even older than the use of chemical agents. The conqueror Hannibal flung clay pots containing poisonous snakes at his enemy during a sea battle in 184 BC. Spaniards during Christopher Columbus's time put the blood of lepers in wine and offered it to French troops to make them ill. The idea of using toxic substances to render an enemy incapable of fighting has existed almost as long as the concept of war.

Types of Biological Agents

Whereas chemical agents are human-made compounds or formulas, biological agents occur naturally. They can kill or paralyze people, kill animals, or destroy crops—all of which may be within the goals of a terrorist organization. Like chemical agents, biological agents can be inhaled, absorbed through the skin, or ingested. There are three main weapons-grade types of biological agents.

1. **Bacteria** Bacteria are microscopic organisms that exist all around us. They cause diseases that can be treated with antibiotics. Initially, anthrax was a disease that was detected in livestock, but it also affects humans. Anthrax (which is caused by a spore-forming bacterium) is almost always fatal when inhaled.

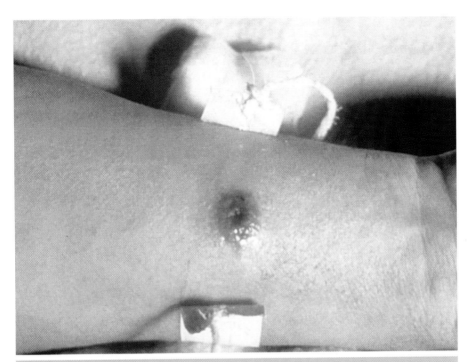

An example of a lesion caused by cutaneous anthrax. Doctors will typically prescribe antibiotics to treat someone infected with anthrax. According to the Centers for Disease Control and Prevention, cutaneous anthrax can result in death if left untreated. However, cutaneous anthrax is the least dangerous form of the disease.

Cutaneous anthrax, which is less often lethal, is characterized by red bumps on the skin that develop into open sores with black centers. Inhaled anthrax can seem like a case of the flu at first, but it leads to a high fever and breathing problems. In later stages, it can spread to the brain.

2. **Viruses** Viruses are 1/100 the size of bacteria and cannot be treated with antibiotics. Only antivirus medicines or immunizations can fight them. One of the more well-known viruses is smallpox. Before smallpox was

eradicated through vaccinations in the 1970s, it was responsible for at least 300 million deaths worldwide in the 3,000 years of its known existence. Thirty percent of smallpox victims die from the disease. It is characterized by flulike symptoms and a reddish rash. Spots from the rash fill with fluid and spread over a victim's body. Smallpox is extremely contagious—it can even be transmitted through contact with the bedsheets of an infected person.

3. **Biological toxins** These are basically poisons that are taken from living things, such as plants, animals, and bacteria. An example of a biological toxin is botulin, a very lethal toxin created by the botulinum bacterium. Botulin causes paralysis and death. In smaller concentrations, it is used in Botox, a cosmetic form of botulin that is used to paralyze the face and reduce the appearance of wrinkles. In a stronger form, botulin is probably one of the deadliest substances on Earth.

Biological agents are generally more deadly than chemical agents, since it usually takes much less of them to cause an equal amount of damage. Additionally, there are many more biological agents than chemical agents on the planet.

How Biological Agents Are Used

Biological agents can be delivered in a number of ways. Like chemical agents, they can be spread through aerosols or through the contamination of food and water supplies.

Unlike chemical agents, however, biological agents are most effective when they linger in the air and are hence easily inhaled. They also present an additional problem since some of the diseases they carry are contagious and can be spread by person-to-person contact.

Is a Biological Attack Likely?

The most likely type of biological attack would be one using either the smallpox virus or the anthrax bacterium, since they are two of the deadliest agents that exist. In 2001, four anthrax-laced letters sent through the mail resulted in two deaths and twenty-three cases of anthrax infection. This use of anthrax as a weapon furthered the sense that biological agents are indeed a real threat.

Biological agents might be chosen by terrorists because the lag time from exposure to symptoms can be anywhere from one day to two weeks. This gives the person delivering the disease an opportunity to escape. A drawback to the use of biological agents is their sensitivity to heat, light, and temperature. With the exception of the anthrax

Letter to Tom Brokaw

Letter to Senator Daschle

These envelopes were contaminated with anthrax. They were mailed in October 2001 to various politicians and members of the media. Several people died after inhaling anthrax spores.

bacterium, many agents can lose their potency when exposed to the elements.

Using biological agents is very expensive and also requires a great deal of knowledge and time. Even if an organization were to develop a biological weapon, delivering it would still be difficult.

The United States has cultures of the smallpox virus in addition to other deadly viruses, bacteria, and toxins for research. These substances are under very strict control and are guarded securely.

How to Handle a Biological Attack

Although we cannot predict when a biological attack will occur, we can take some basic preventive measures in case one does. Making sure you are up to date for any required immunizations is a good first step. Installing a high efficiency particulate air (HEPA) filter in your home may also prevent certain biological agents from entering your home and lingering. HEPA filters are very powerful air filters that can cleanse a room of particles that cannot even be seen by the naked eye. HEPA filters can remove up to 99.97 percent of small particles in a room. The filters in a HEPA device must be changed frequently for maximum efficiency.

Since identifying that a biological attack has taken place may be difficult, vigilance may prove to be very important. Don't forget your emergency plan! Having a basic first response in your mind may reduce your chances of being seriously affected by an attack.

Warning signs of the release of an agent are similar to the indicators that signal a chemical attack. These can

Air filters are an effective defense against biological agents. The industrial-sized HEPA filtration system shown in the background was installed at a military site. The smaller air filters seen in the inset are designed to be used in home furnaces. These filters can also remove common particles like dust mites and pet dander that aggravate allergies .

include strange odors, clouds of smoke or vapor, and the onset of symptoms in others around you. Strange unattended packages near sources of air (such as air intakes for heating and cooling systems) should be treated with some suspicion. If any of these are apparent, use good sense and leave the area, keeping upwind of the possible threat. Seeking high ground is not advisable, since biological agents tend to float. Notify authorities, and listen to the radio or check a local news channel for news updates. As we've mentioned, evidence of a biological attack may not be immediately obvious, so remain where

A man is showered for decontamination during a 2004 Emergency Management Agency drill in Pennsylvania. Emergency personnel from seven counties used the drill to test their response to a terrorist attack. Drills like these are also used to prepare for other emergencies, such as chemical spills and weather disasters.

you are until you are informed that your environment is safe.

If you think that you have been exposed to a biological agent, remove your clothing and anything you may be carrying and seal it in a plastic bag for disposal. Decontaminate yourself as best you can, showering thoroughly with antibacterial soap. Tell a parent or guardian what is going on. If you develop general symptoms, contact a doctor, but do not travel unless you are advised to do so. If an illness can be transmitted from person to person (smallpox, for instance), one may need to be quarantined or put in isolation to prevent a disease from spreading.

Being prepared for an emergency is very important, but don't let the mere possibility of such an event control your life. Remember, your odds of getting in a traffic accident are much higher than being attacked by terrorists. A sore throat and headache don't always mean that you have been exposed to a dangerous biological agent. You may simply be catching a cold. The advice and steps outlined here shouldn't make you more fearful—they are designed to help you remain clearheaded and calm in case the worst happens.

6 --- Nuclear and Radiological Attacks

Nuclear and radiological attacks present the greatest threat known to man. The scale of destruction and injury they can cause is so large that one attack could change the course of history. Unlike other types of terrorist attacks, a nuclear or radiological attack can affect millions of people over thousands of miles and for dozens of years.

What Are Nuclear and Radiological Devices?

On a very basic level, a nuclear bomb creates an explosion; however, that explosion is almost impossible to imagine. The detonation of a nuclear device can be viewed as four deadly attacks in one. Along with the extreme light and heat a nuclear device creates, harmful gamma rays are released, in addition to a powerful shock wave and winds reaching hundreds of miles per hour. The power unleashed by a nuclear device is unparalleled—even a moderately sized nuclear weapon could destroy an entire city.

Another result of a nuclear detonation is an electro-magnetic pulse (EMP), which can disrupt electrical devices. An EMP can extend for thousands of miles and destroy all electrical and computer equipment in its path. An EMP would severely hurt rescue attempts, since phones, computers, aircraft, and communications technology could be rendered useless.

Nuclear blasts also create fallout, or radioactive particles that can be more deadly than any chemical or biological agent. Fallout can usually only be detected with special equipment—it often cannot be seen and has no odor. Fallout not only affects people inside of a nuclear blast, but it can also be carried by the wind and distributed around the world. Exposure to fallout can result in diseases and ailments, such as cancer, caused by radiation.

A radiological device contains nuclear material, but does not create a nuclear explosion. Instead radiological devices

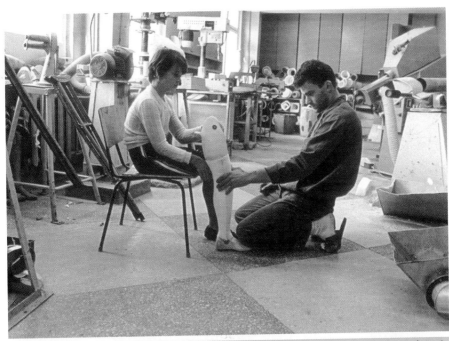

A young victim of the Chernobyl nuclear disaster is fitted for a prosthetic leg. A massive explosion rocked the Chernobyl nuclear power plant in the Soviet Union on April 26, 1986. The catastrophe released enormous amounts of radiation into the surrounding areas, which resulted in an increase in birth defects, hereditary diseases, and genetic mutations.

fit into the category of unconventional explosive devices that contain radioactive material instead of glass or metal. A more common name for a device such as this is a "dirty bomb" or a "dirty nuke." A dirty bomb will not cause as much destruction as a nuclear bomb or warhead, but will still harm a great number of people inside and outside of the blast area.

How Nuclear or Radiological Devices Are Used

The strength of nuclear devices differs according to the power of the weapon and the altitude of the blast. A high-altitude blast results in less fallout, but a wider area can be affected by the initial explosion. If two nations at war used nuclear weapons against each other, they would most likely launch them at one another and find the altitude to detonate that would cause the most damage. As far as terrorists and terrorist groups are concerned, launching nuclear weapons is not a practical option. A more probable scenario would involve a terrorist group detonating a small nuclear device or a dirty bomb that could fit into a suitcase or a small vehicle. The radioactive material used do not need to be "pure" for a dirty bomb—it could be radioactive waste from a power plant.

Terrorists could also bomb or otherwise sabotage a nuclear power plant. Besides the damage that such an attack might cause, it could also result in massive blackouts.

Is a Nuclear or Radiological Attack Likely?

While a nuclear or radiological attack is less likely than any other acts of terrorism, it still remains a possibility. These types of attacks are attractive to terrorists not only for the immense amount of damage they can cause, but also because of the fear and chaos they can create. Although nuclear materials are difficult to acquire in the United States, some countries do not have as strict controls on their power facilities and nuclear storage. It is fair to say that as long as radioactive material exists, the potential for its use in an explosive device cannot be ruled out.

Steam is seen rising from a tube leak at the Indian Point nuclear facility in Westchester County, New York, in February 2000. Indian Point is often mentioned as a potential terrorist target because of its proximity to New York City.

Nonetheless, obtaining a nuclear weapon would be a very difficult task for terrorist groups to accomplish. As far as building a nuclear device, the expense and technical expertise required are relatively high but not out of reach. Also, the materials needed to make a full-scale nuclear device can pose a serious health risk to its builders. Even if a bomb were built and didn't detonate properly, it would become a kind of dirty bomb that would still be capable of causing tremendous damage. Of the two options, a dirty bomb is much more likely to be used for terrorism than a conventional nuclear warhead.

How to Handle a Nuclear or Radiological Attack

Sadly, anyone within the blast radius of a full-fledged nuclear attack will most likely not survive. This could be anywhere from a few city blocks to six or seven miles (ten or eleven kilometers). People outside this area (depending on the distance) will have to deal with a multitude of dangers. The destruction brought about by a nuclear device will likely be widespread, including fires, third-degree burns, and unsafe or collapsed buildings. Fallout is also a major consideration after a nuclear attack. It can be extremely life threatening, but its effects can be lessened depending on proximity to adequate shelter, distance from the blast center, and time itself. Some of the advice discussed in chapter 3 will prove very useful in planning for the aftermath of the detonation of a nuclear device.

Preparing for and coping with a nuclear attack may be slightly more involved than doing so for other threats, such as a hurricane or other natural disaster. For example, an emergency kit for a nuclear attack should include a two-week supply of food and water.

Finding proper shelter is another consideration. As part of your emergency plan, you should know the location of the nearest blast shelter. You can find this information from your local chamber of commerce. A blast shelter provides some defense against the light, heat, and powerful winds

A Virginia man assists his wife in entering their fallout shelter. Interest in fallout shelters has surged since the September 11 terrorist attacks. Food, medical supplies, oxygen tanks, and battery-operated radios are some things you might find in a fallout shelter. These shelters can also offer protection from tornadoes and hurricanes.

that a nuclear explosion can bring. As for the resulting fallout, you should also know where one or more fallout shelters are in your neighborhood or near your school. Some shelters are specifically designed to protect against fallout, but any structure that can absorb the majority of radiation given off by a nuclear device can serve as a fallout shelter. Depending on your distance from the blast, you may have to remain in a fallout or blast shelter for an indeterminate amount of time.

BE INFORMED
NUCLEAR BLAST

Take cover immediately, below ground if possible, though any shield or shelter will help protect you from the immediate effects of the blast and the pressure wave.

Consider if you can get out of the area;

Or if it would be better to go inside a building and follow your plan to "shelter-in-place".

Shielding: If you have a thick shield between yourself and the radioactive materials more of the radiation will be absorbed, and you will be exposed to less.

Distance: The farther away from the blast and the fallout the lower your exposure.

Time: Minimizing time spent exposed will also reduce your risk.

If there is knowledge of a coming attack, there are some additional steps you can take. First, find an appropriate blast or fallout shelter, even if the explosion occurs many miles away. Ask your teacher or a parent where the nearest shelter is if you're not certain and make note of these locations in your emergency plan. Be sure to find adequate shelter as quickly as possible. Once you are safely inside, do not leave. Listen to the radio to find out what may be happening.

If no warnings are given or you are not indoors when a nuclear attack takes place, FEMA offers some additional advice:

1. Don't look at the explosion. The light and heat are so great they will blind you.

2. Take cover behind anything that will offer protection, such as a cement wall or natural barrier.

3. Lie flat on the ground and stay there. If the explosion is far away, the shock wave could take up to thirty seconds to arrive.

In the event of the use of a radiological device such as a dirty bomb, the destruction may not be as widespread, but the presence of radioactive material will still pose a problem. Unfortunately, since radiation can't be seen, the best option may be to assume that an explosion may contain it. Treat this scenario in the same way you would react to the release of biological or chemical weapons. If you happen to be outdoors, leave the area and get upwind of the explosion as you head to the nearest shelter. If you were close to the

BE INFORMED
RADIATION THREAT

A radiation threat or "Dirty Bomb" is the use of common explosives to spread radioactive materials.

It is not a nuclear blast. The force of the explosion and radioactive contamination will be more localized. In order to limit the amount of radiation you are exposed to, think about shielding, distance and time.

Shielding: If you have a thick shield between yourself and the radioactive materials more of the radiation will be absorbed by the thick shield, and you will be exposed to less.

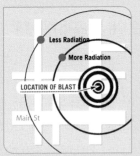

Distance: The farther away you are from the radiation the lower your exposure.

Time: Minimizing time spent exposed will also reduce your risk.

Local authorities may not be able to immediately provide information on what is happening and what you should do. However, you should watch TV, listen to the radio, or check the Internet often for official news and information as it becomes available.

site of an attack and exposed to radiation, symptoms would not be immediately apparent. Find shelter and perform the same actions you would if you were definitely exposed. Keep your hands away from your face and mouth to reduce the chances of dangerous materials entering your body. If you can, take off your clothing and personal items, and wash yourself thoroughly with soap and water. Do not leave the shelter until you are told it is safe to do so.

If a dirty bomb or similar device is detonated and you are indoors, do your best to prevent any radioactivity from reaching you. Close or seal up any windows, fireplaces, and doors. You can use the duct tape in your emergency kit to seal doors or other openings. Be aware that plastic will not stop radiation.

In addition, any and all heating and cooling systems should be turned off. Go to the safest place in the house or building. This will be a room with very few windows (if any), and as much protection as possible between you and the outside. As in any emergency of this type, do not judge for yourself when it is safe to go outside. Stay tuned to the radio and wait for further instructions from adults or other officials.

Be Prepared

Although the prospect of a terrorist attack is undoubtedly frightening, that same fear can be helpful in dealing with the possibility of such an event. Remember, terrorists attack not only physical targets, but psychological ones as well. People who have survived serious attacks in Tokyo, Oklahoma City, and New York City have all had to find ways to go on with their lives following these horrific events.

Fear is an essential component of terrorist strikes. The most important thing you can do is try to balance your fear with common sense and preparedness. After the attacks of September 11, New York City mayor Rudy Giuliani and other officials urged the citizens of New York to try to return to their normal lives as soon as possible. Neglecting daily routines and remaining fearful of another strike serve very little purpose. Since we can never know the time and place of an attack, our best defense is to understand what methods of attack terrorists may use, and to have a firm plan of action to help survive and cope afterward.

The tools presented in this book provide a basic framework for essential emergency preparation. The additional Web sites and resources listed in the back of this book supply even more advice on how to become more aware of the threats and challenges that can exist in our world, and how to meet them every day.

Glossary

anthrax An often fatal disease caused by spores of the bacterium *Bacillus anthracis*. The disease is normally transmitted by human contact with infected animal skin or feces.

asphyxiant An organic or man-made agent that causes suffocation.

cardiopulmonary resuscitation (CPR) A first-aid procedure performed on a person who has suffered a cardiac arrest.

decontamination The process of removing harmful radioactive, chemical, or biological material from a person or object.

dirty bomb The term given to a radiological dispersion device (RDD) that combines radioactive material with a conventional bomb.

fallout Particles of debris found in the air and ground following a nuclear blast.

incapacitate To disable or make weaker.

radioactivity Particles, rays, and waves given off by radioactive material, such as nuclear waste, plutonium, and uranium.

spore A small heat- and weather-resistant organism that can spawn a new organism.

terrorism The use of force or violence by a group or an individual in order to bend another group to its will, which is usually political or ideological.

Threat Advisory Level A color-coded alert developed by the U.S. Department of Homeland Security that indicates the risk of a terrorist attack.

toxin A poisonous substance produced by living organisms such as bacteria and viruses.

For More Information

American Red Cross National Headquarters
2025 E Street NW
Washington, DC 20006
(202) 303-4498
Web site: http://www.redcross.org

Centers for Disease Control and Prevention (CDC)
1600 Clifton Road
Atlanta, GA 30333
(404) 639-3311
Web site: http://www.cdc.gov

Department of Homeland Security
Washington, DC 20528
(202) 282-8000
Web site: http://www.dhs.gov

Federal Emergency Management Association (FEMA)
500 C Street SW
Washington, DC 20472
(202) 566-1600
Web site: http://www.fema.gov

Web Sites

Due to the changing nature of Internet links, the Rosen Publishing Group, Inc., has developed an online list of Web sites related to the subject of this book. This site is updated regularly. Please use this link to access the list:

http://www.rosenlinks.com/lep/teat

For Further Reading

Alexander, David. *Principles of Emergency Planning and Management*. Oxford, England: Oxford University Press, 2002.

Croddy, Eric, Clarisa Perez-Armendariz, and John Hart. *Chemical and Biological Warfare: Comprehensive Survey for the Concerned Citizen*. New York, NY: Springer, 2001.

Davis, Lynn E., Tom LaTourrette, David Mosher, Lois Davis, and David Howell. *What You Should Do to Prepare for and Respond to Chemical, Radiological, Nuclear, and Biological Terrorist Attacks: Pocket Edition Survival Guide*. Available for download only (http://www.rand.org/publications/MR/MR1731.2).

Hasan, Tahara. *Anthrax Attacks Around the World*. New York, NY: Rosen Publishing, 2003.

Kerrigan, Michael. *Biological and Germ Warfare Protection*. Broomal, PA: Mason Crest Publishers, 2003.

Laquer, Walter and Walter Reich. *Origins of Terrorism: Psychologies, Ideologies, Theologies, States of Mind*. Washington, D.C.: Woodrow Wilson Center Press, 1998.

Margulies, Phillip. *Al Qaeda: Osama Bin Laden's Army of Terrorists*. New York, NY: Rosen Publishing, 2003.

National Commission on Terrorist Attacks. *The 9/11 Commission Report: Final Report of the National*

Commission on Terrorist Attacks Upon the United States. New York, NY: W. W. Norton and Company, 2004.

Poolos, J. *The Nerve Gas Attack on the Tokyo Subway.* New York, NY: Rosen Publishing, 2003.

Bibliography

Allison, Graham. *Nuclear Terrorism: The Ultimate Preventable Catastrophe*. New York, NY: Times Books, 2004.

Carr, Caleb. *The Lessons of Terror: A History of Warfare Against Civilians: Why It Has Always Failed and Why It Will Fail Again*. New York, NY: Random House, 2002.

Cooper, Paul W., and Stanley R. Kurowski. *Introduction to the Technology of Explosions*. New York, NY: Wiley VCH, 1997.

Crenshaw, Martha. *Terrorism in Context*. University Park, PA: Penn State Press, 1995.

Croddy, Eric, Clarisa Perez-Armendariz, and John Hart. *Chemical and Biological Warfare: Comprehensive Survey for the Concerned Citizen*. New York, NY: Springer, 2001.

Federal Emergency Management Association. *Are You Ready? An In-Depth Guide to Citizen Preparedness*. FEMA Pub H-34, Revised September 2002.

Hutchinson, Robert. *Weapons of Mass Destruction: The No-Nonsense Guide to Nuclear, Chemical, and Biological Weapons Today*. London, England: George Weidenfeld and Nicholson, 2003.

National Commission on Terrorist Attacks. *The 9/11 Commission Report: Final Report of the National Commission on Terrorist Attacks Upon the United States*. New York, NY: W. W. Norton and Company, 2004.

Preston, Richard. *The Hot Zone: A Terrifying True Story*. New York, NY: Anchor Books, 1995.

Index

About the Author

Kerry Hinton is a writer who lives and works in Hoboken, New Jersey.

Photo Credits

Cover, pp. 1, 5, 15, 20, 27, 28, 39, 41, 42, 47, 49 © AP/Wide World Photos; p. 8 © Greg Smith/Corbis; p. 11 http://www.dhs.gov/dhspublic/interapp/editorial_0566.xml; p. 12, 22, 23, 24, 32, 34, 50, 52 courtesy of the United States Department of Homeland Security; p. 29 © Corbis/Sygma; p. 37 courtesy of the Department of Health and Human Services, Centers for Disease Control and Prevention; p. 41 (inset) © Syracuse Newspapers/Dick Blume/The Image Works; p. 45 © A. Kleschuk/Corbis Sygma.

Designer: Tahara Hasan
Editor: Christine Poolos